Bon appétit!

Todd

Tuesday's Muse

Visual & Verbal Appetizers for the
Great Banquet of Your Life

Contents

Acknowledgments

Poets and pastors rarely have scheduled work hours. A muse refuses to punch the clock. I am grateful for the patience of my family over the years – my wife, Jennie; and my children: Katie, Holly, and Owen – who've put up with the countless interruptions of inspirational moments, as words, phrases, and ideas were written on scraps of paper or typed into text-messages in the middle of meals, conversations, and family outings.

All but one of these poems/prayers were written while I was (and still am) serving the congregation at First Presbyterian Church, Fayetteville, Tennessee. Over the past 17+ years, this congregation and I have been through some dark valleys and across some spectacular mountaintops. In listening to and praying through their lives and circumstances and mine, I have come to better understand how we are meant to live in community; and how our presence, conversations, and words help define that life.

Though these poems/prayers surely come from many years of distilling and marinating, it is often a particular time, place, and circumstance that squeeze the words onto page and screen in a form that gives meaning. I am eternally grateful to the members of this congregation and community for allowing me to grow with them, across life's ebb and flow.

This project would never have gotten off the ground without the people who encouraged me, providing editorial comments and proofreading: Anne Apple, Pat Hallum, and Terri Taylor. I also could not have put together this collection without the wonderful cover design by Susan Moore Graham, the formatting help of Ben Alford and Andi Birdsong, and the powerful photographic contributions of friends and relatives: Cyndi Crafton Bagley, Kay Campbell, Lesedi Chambers, Jessi Higginbotham, Holly Jane Jenkins, Jennie Roberts Jenkins, Katie Jenkins Kester, Lee Lindsey McKinney, Janet Tuck, and Adam Valencia (Huntsville Immigration Initiative LLC).

Introduction

Poetry is about blank space, pauses, and silence, as much as it is about words. It gives the readers enough of a taste of the poet's thoughts, ideas, feelings, and experiences to draw them in; but leaves them a little bit hungry, both allowing and requiring them to finish the meal with their own words, ideas, emotions, and stories. Sometimes, my poetry is a distillation process, beginning with a verse of five, six, or more lines; each succeeding verse containing one less line than the preceding one; the final verse a single line of hope, distilled. Once I noticed this pattern, I wrote "Distillery" as a way to understand this particular form. My prayer is that the appetizers in this book will encourage you to find, distill, enjoy, and share the banquet of your own life.

The first time I ever wrote a poem was November 24, 1994. My wife, our three children, and I were spending Thanksgiving with her aunt, Emma Rossman, in Albany, Georgia. I was experiencing sermon-block that week, and the time with family and away from home and church, I hoped, would help me figure out what/how to preach on Sunday. In my mind, it was a particularly momentous Sunday for at least two reasons: [1] it was the First Sunday of Advent; and [2] unbeknownst to the members of my congregation, a Pastor Nominating (search) Committee from another congregation was coming to hear me preach.

As our enjoyable and delicious Thanksgiving lunch was finishing, I suddenly had a flash of inspiration. While my family cleared and left the table, I picked up my napkin and a pen, quickly writing, before the words left me. In my mind, I could hear and feel the cadence of Clement Moore's poem, "The Night Before Christmas" and the words that were coming to me were about how the church struggles with and through Advent. After the napkin was filled with verses, I went to a quiet place and finished the piece on the back of a scrap piece of paper.

When Sunday came, I was less-than confident because, in addition to the two abovementioned circumstances, my sermon was nothing more than this poem – the only poem I'd ever written! I had no idea if it would speak to the congregation at all, and wasn't exactly sure how to introduce it. I could not bring myself to come right out and say, "I wrote this poem, and I want to share it with you." I remember thinking, "That just doesn't sound like something I would say." mostly because I could not imagine myself as a poet. I muddled through an introduction that was quite incoherent, and then slowly read the poem.

After worship, I went out to lunch with the visiting Pastor Nominating Committee and had an informal interview with them. My conversation with this PNC never progressed beyond that day. Years later, I became friends with one of the members of that committee. I don't remember exactly how, but the topic of the PNC's process and their consideration of me came up in a conversation once. He told me that, on the ride home that Sunday afternoon, one of the members of the committee said, "I don't know why we would call him as our pastor; his whole sermon was just a poem, and he didn't even tell us who wrote it!"

Note to self: Claim your work!

Isaiah 43:18-21 Do not remember the former things, or consider the things of old. 19 I am about to do a new thing; now it springs forth, do you not perceive it? I will make a way in the wilderness and rivers in the desert. 20 The wild animals will honor me, the jackals and the ostriches; for I give water in the wilderness, rivers in the desert, to give drink to my chosen people, 21 the people whom I formed for myself so that they might declare my praise.

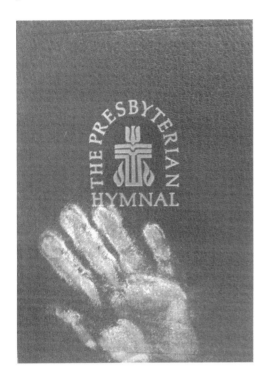

Holy Hoarding

Reeling from a loss both real
and imagined, trumped-up and palpable,
she clutches programs and possessions,
discarding connections and relationships,
 sure of only two things:

everything in the past was better;
nothing in the future will be as worthy;
 not because she is shallow or selfish,
but because pain is so disorienting,

that her grieving heart cannot
fathom surviving another loss.

As the publications and furniture pile up,
space for her children diminishes.
History's inventory and cataloging
have become a consuming fire;
room at the table shrinks.

Stacking stones against a sea
of change, not seeing that all mortar
is a futile attempt to capture freedom,
and rigidity leaves no room for beauty or
for tide to sweep us toward the Universe;
avoiding the deeps where grace
shines as the only path toward hope.

Who knew that her groom's absence
would expose such vulnerability?
Whose idea was it to send
unpredictable sister in his stead?

Don't think for a minute
that you will do any better.
Pray for the day when
the whole family comes back;

not to indulge her for
another holiday ritual
whose power has faded
like old Polaroids in the sun,
as method is mistaken for message;

but to profess undying love
and wholehearted commitment
to yard sales, until there is room
for all generations at the table,
so bread and wine may once again

seal water's covenant blessing.

Until that dawning arrives,
hopeful sister-in-law hovers heart to heart,
fanning long-gray coals with truth
that time and space cannot contain.

She is our mother, our sister.
She is our church.

Matthew 11:28-30 "Come to me, all you that are weary and are carrying heavy burdens, and I will give you rest. 29 Take my yoke upon you, and learn from me; for I am gentle and humble in heart, and you will find rest for your souls. 30 For my yoke is easy, and my burden is light."

Dance of the Caregiver

Mirror of life reflects the paradox
of a caring so soft and tender
yet so strong and exhausting;
overwhelming compassion that

wrenches you in the deep places;
drains your own spirit in the
process of caring for others;
filling you with emptiness.

You reach the place where
running on nothing seems to be
the way it was meant to be

but at the center of who you are

you know better; know that
empty hearts like exhausted hands
cannot hold and serve with the
same love and care as full, rested ones.

Souls athirst will not be quenched
from a well that has run dry;
babes will be denied hunger's relief
at a breast that has no milk.

Immerse your life in fallowness,
replenish your fields' nutrients
so the crop of your healing gift
may yield its bumper harvest.

Go to the table where rest and food
nourish your capacity to nourish;
feed the very core of your being;
fan your coal of life to flaming hope.

Esther 4:13-14 Mordecai told them to reply to Esther, "Do not think that in the king's palace you will escape any more than all the other Jews. 14 For if you keep silence at such a time as this, relief and deliverance will rise for the Jews from another quarter, but you and your father's family will perish. Who knows? Perhaps you have come to royal dignity for just such a time as this."

Plans

We make them every day;
change them within hours;
scrap them in minutes when
the comedy of errors collapses.

The one who dreamed of stardom,
wowing fans in the sports arena,
saw that dream end in injury;
went to medical school instead.

The would-be world traveler
came into a home and family
void of extravagant resources;
went to nursing school instead.

The Wall Street trader wanna be
now knows how lucky he was as he
floundered in that financial hope;
became a hospital administrator instead.

The one who still dreams of law school,
has yet to put together the necessary mix
of grades, grants, and recommendations;
keeps the dream alive as medical support staff.

The one whose career and family goals
may appear to be playing second fiddle
to maniacal physical fitness;
only knows that it's a driving force.

The little boy, whose dreams for now
still full of innocence and simplicity,
doesn't yet know that those aspirations
will blossom and bear much fruit.

Others feel a single dream
long before words can describe it;
self-applied Olympic hopefuls
devoting a lifetime toward the journey.

We best not fool ourselves, believing
that dreams are only for the glamorous.
Every cog propels the flow
of our collective downstream journey.

Conductor of our dream orchestra
patiently brings together our aggregate plans,
forever re-writing the opus' score until
chords of hope complete our lives.

Mark 9:36-37 Then he took a little child and put it among them; and taking it in his arms, he said to them, 37 "Whoever welcomes one such child in my name welcomes me, and whoever welcomes me welcomes not me but the one who sent me."

Inner Child

Journey to the center of who you are;
there you will meet the young one:
child of innocence, hope and expectation,
of creativity, playfulness and imagination.

Life often grinds on the child within,
squeezing, bending, twisting, hemming in;
elusive happiness supplants pure joy;
supple grape of youth turns into yesteryear's raisin.

Where trust is betrayed, purity violated,
where love is withdrawn, affirmation withheld,
young one slinks toward the periphery,
leaving us to believe the child is no more.

There in the shadows, against the wall,
youth waits and hopes, because nothing else matters.

"Tell me I'm special; tell me you care.
Speak tenderly of the worth of my being."

More often than not, the words never come;
time creates an adult who pushes forward.
Children may come to bring their gift,
but all we see is another imperfection.

Facade of self-confidence, ego blustering,
all the while feeling like less and less,
spewing the angry shrapnel of dysfunction
into the face of all who dare intimacy.

Grace steps in to deliver her mystery,
gently summoning from the deepest places
the very words we've ached so long to hear;
we whisper them first into the child's ear.

Unleashing the power of their glory and nakedness,
they open us all to the tender love story
we heard before we were born, but seem to have forgotten,
spoken by the One who gave us breath.

In passing them on lies the possibility
of finally claiming them for ourselves;
Grace's gift comes, not from without,
but from deep places where the child plays.

Genesis 2: 7 then the Lord God formed man from the dust of the ground, and breathed into his nostrils the breath of life; and the man became a living being.

Breath

It's such a simple thing,
almost forgettable second nature;
involuntary reflex that keeps
oxygen flowing in, CO_2 out,

until something goes awry;
neurotransmitters lose their way,
internal traffic snarl creates
need for emergency measures.

Long lost are links between
Hebrew and Greek meanings:
spirit, breath, wind, all a single word
requiring contextual interpretation.

As ventilator pumps its steady cadence,
three meanings are reconnected;

prayers waft heavenward asking
God to blow once more.

Across the face of chaotic deep
where worlds and life collide
into the sails of human spirit
call—no cry—for impetus erupts:

You, giver of all that
every language's meaning holds,
send your gift anew
that we may marvel at your grace!

Psalm 130:3-4 If you, O Lord, should mark iniquities, Lord, who could stand? 4 But there is forgiveness with you, so that you may be revered.

Excuses

Excuses: the peripheral events
we push to the forefront in an attempt
to lessen the impact of our choices
and avoid some of the responsibility
for all the words and actions
used and taken, withheld and neglected.

Everyone has extenuating circumstances
in their life that, when carefully
stacked with reason and mortared with intent,

build a one-sided wall that looks
impenetrable from the inside,
 yet altogether like
the emperor's new clothes
from the out.

Integrity in relationship comes
when periphery remains at the margins,
penitence comes from the heart,
hope flows from the promise
to learn, love, and live
toward a tomorrow where
second chances are genuine and
relationships are valued above scores.

Matthew 26:38-39 Then he said to them, "I am deeply grieved, even to death; remain here, and stay awake with me." 39 And going a little farther, he threw himself on the ground and prayed, "My Father, if it is possible, let this cup pass from me; yet not what I want but what you want."

Passion

Purple tells the story straight-up,
blending the crimson of life with
the blue of oxygen depletion;
a life spent, completely used.

Somewhere in the night
a heart beats for love,
not control or selfishness
but for voluntary self-emptying;

heart that has been lanced
by human ignorance, bruised
by vested interest's shield, shaken
by indifference's arrhythmia.

Words have run their course,
reached the limit of their effect;
silence is broken only by
the escalating pound of percussion.

Sleep comes to the ignorant
who perceive they are innocent;
anguish washes the garden
in its agitating pallor.

Power and politics close in,
control and religion close behind;
love's dangerous offer of vulnerability
once again proves too risky.

The donkey-propelled grand marshal
of Sunday's palm parade has now become
the prize catch of Jerusalem's finest,
in every sense of the word.

The life that will be taken is freely offered,
not to appease an angry deity,
or to demonstrate love's deep recesses,
but to rescue us to the path to deliverance.

Matthew 4:1-2 Then Jesus was led up by the Spirit into the wilderness to be tempted by the devil. 2 He fasted forty days and forty nights, and afterwards he was famished.

Forty Days

Come away with me for a while
to wilderness, desert, or your own neighborhood;
the journey inward is littered with temporal securities,
tossed aside as their worth is examined.

With each letting go comes a mixture
of anxiety and relief, fear and release;
that on which our safety seems propped
faces the dare of letting go, letting down.

Long-time companions are still around,
word and silence, listening and breath;
but our reliance on them has been relegated

to moments of crisis, matters of chaos.

Our suburban securities sufficiently strewn,
the invitation is to reacquaint ourselves
with the basic tools of faithful living,
daring us to trust simplicity again, for the first time.

Sound of the beating heart emerges,
rhythm of measured breathing settles in,
holy words slowly wash over stillness,
graceful Otherness bubbles to the surface.

The only path that leads to resurrection
takes us through the purple haze of pain,
leads us in the dance of suffering,
nails us to the tree of unliving.

The empty tomb cannot be reached
unless we dare to bare ourselves
to rigor mortis' relentless march,
before the rising sun of grace's throne.

John 11:43-44 When he had said this, he cried with a loud voice, "Lazarus, come out!" 44 The dead man came out, his hands and feet bound with strips of cloth, and his face wrapped in a cloth. Jesus said to them, "Unbind him, and let him go."

Home

Prayer is uttered here and now
about your journey home.
The road is long and often hard;
you never walk alone.

God's peace that passes understanding
hold you safe and sound.
May you be wrapped in tenderness
with loving arms around.

As grace enfolds you like a glove
and mercy's blankets spread,
may all your pain and cares be gone;
each and every dread;

forgiveness soothe you like a salve,
each weight rise as a cloud;

joy be everlasting as
your name is called aloud.

Hebrews 10:22 ...let us approach with a true heart in full assurance of faith, with our hearts sprinkled clean from an evil conscience and our bodies washed with pure water.

Innocents

Ever notice how God
never dwells on blame?
Yet it's a powerful tool of self-destruction
and the beginning of the end
for many fragile relationships.

When guilt is allowed to overshadow grace,
everything that God intends is subverted;
as if knowing whom to blame, self or others,
will change the way we think and feel
or turn back the clock somehow.

It cannot be the will of God
for the innocents to suffer
or those who love them
to accept the burden
of what's beyond their control.

When evil falls like acid rain
and scorches tender skin,
I curse the pain, wail in grief,
and shout before the hill,
"Come down from that cross,

hold this child in tender arms
and breathe your spirit deep
into this family's broken heart!
Stop the clock – yea, turn it back,
and Lazarus us once more!"

Psalm 45:17 I will perpetuate your memory through all generations; therefore the nations will praise you forever and ever. (NIV)

Auld Lang Syne

It's just an illusion to help us
think we have control of
our lives, the world, you know –
this calendar counting,
time measuring thing we do –
days, weeks, months, years, centuries.

Digits help us keep track of
events, places, people who have
cursed or graced our paths with
their rhythmic breathing,
metronomic, tic-tocking lives.

This year fades into next;
faces and places blend into
an oatmeal gruel of tasteless memory,
if we focus only on
the names and numbers.

But when it's eyes and smiles we file away,
and joyous moments on the way,
when time stands still and sunlight
bathes our hearts with joy too deep for words,
then years and faces, names and
places become the insignificant
backdrop against which grace paints.

So when I see your eyes aglow and
catch that fox-sly grin, I'll surely know
you're passing on to me
a priceless loving memory
of what life's purpose is meant to be.
I'll file it away so I can share it too,
someday, when love becomes
the only measure.

Luke 24:30-31 When he was at the table with them, he took bread, blessed and broke it, and gave it to them. 31 Then their eyes were opened, and they recognized him; and he vanished from their sight.

Left in the Lurch

Knowing reaches into the future,
not as far as we'd like, but
something is better than nothing;
memory and hope must somehow intersect.

Information comes at us in fits and starts.
Life's puzzle is in infinite pieces,
doesn't arrive all at once in a box;
sometimes we're sure some major pieces are lost.

Good news sometimes, bad news others.
Mostly somewhere in-between,
whose final determination must wait
for more time to pass, paths to cross.

It's hurry up and wait most of the time,
arriving at a known milestone,
waiting for the journey's next leg to appear.
"Recalculating" is life's operative word.

Memories not only of knowledge gained,
but also of futures planned,
sunsets and evenings, new days dawning,
all hang in the balance as earth and sky touch.

Hope: once simple, pure, and light;
now queasy from life's roller coaster;
whole-grain heavy, fibrous husks and all;
certainly different but more substantial.

Feed us from the heart, O Lord,
of your promise lived-in-skin;
richness and depth of hope that is
broken-in and not broken-down.

Psalm 34:8 O taste and see that the Lord is good; happy are those who take refuge in him.

Sensing

To the House of Holy Grudge,
I believe that I must say,
though I looked far and wide,
I did not see your God today.

To the Sanctuary of the Sacred Scorekeeper,
I think that I must say,
though I heard high and low,
I did not hear your God today.

To the Cathedral of the Punishing Parent,
I must confess and say,
though I smelled from east to west,
I did not smell your God today.

To the Church of the Divine Tyrant,
I know that I must say,

though I touched from north to south,
I did not touch your God today.

To the Spirit of Mercy, Forgiveness, Grace,
it brings me joy to say,
when I experienced all your gifts,
I tasted Love today.

Jonah 1:3 But Jonah set out to flee to Tarshish from the presence of the Lord. He went down to Joppa and found a ship going to Tarshish; so he paid his fare and went on board, to go with them to Tarshish, away from the presence of the Lord.

As If

"I just want what's
best for me."
he says, firmly convinced
 he has a clue
what that would be.

"My life is NOT going
according to plan!"
her bumper sticker proclaims,
as if an earthly sojourn
tailored by her desires
would be heavenly.

Joy is the journey
of those who, from
sheer exhaustion and failure,
or contemplative acquiescence,

it matters not which,
daily invite holy otherness
to rearrange the cargo
of their dreams and plans.

Theirs is a ship
whose ports are celebrated,
whose manifesto is shape-shifted
by grace into daily manna
from the universe's core
of unconditional love.

John 11:35 Jesus wept. (NIV)

Sinking In

When grande grief is bearing down
upon life unaware,
spirit gives anesthesia
so we can live and bear

pain too great for anyone.
Numbness spreads and covers
a safety net, our heart to hold
bits of loved and lovers

that otherwise would fly away
into the great abyss,
leave us breathless, without hope
for those we dearly miss.

There comes a day with fog so thick
we can't remember how
we walked or even tried to think
beyond the here and now.

As time goes by, feeling returns

and pain becomes so real;
excruciating sensations
beyond our wish to deal.

The promise of the gospel:
that Christ will be our salve;
will take us deep within to where
our love will truly have

the chance for pain to sink into
the growing places where
a person gives the self away
all for the chance to share

love once rooted in
a life no longer here,
but one still kindling flame
that always will be near.

Because this is a pain so deep
its roots will reach a place
anchored in the self of God,
where every breath is grace.

Psalm 100:4-5 Enter his gates with thanksgiving, and his courts with praise. Give thanks to him, bless his name. 5 For the Lord is good; his steadfast love endures forever, and his faithfulness to all generations.

No Less Days

Math done by the holy One
has its own unique formula,
defying all the neat, orderly
equations that frame creation.

Ten thousand years—so long
John Newton could not imagine
its beginning or its end;
used it to define eternity.

Grace, the amazing offering,
becomes the lazy eight,
laying down its very life,
creating mysterious infinity.

Timeless measure + immeasurable gift
define God's limitlessness,

love's overwhelming power;
math that will not let us go.

Forever trumps all counting,
love overcomes all obstacles,
joy the gift that grows larger
each time we give it away.

John 3: 8 The wind blows where it chooses, and you hear the sound of it, but you do not know where it comes from or where it goes. So it is with everyone who is born of the Spirit."

Destination

Cloud of self-important dust flying
racing pell-mell toward somewhere,
a place long ago identified.
Bumper sticker reads: Utopia or bust.

G.P.S. locked into target,
portfolio planned to perfection;
minimal stops, maximum speed;
pity the fool who stands in the way.

Detour ahead, reduce speed;
slow for sheep crossing,
bridge out, turn around;
gully washer terminates travel.

Panic sets in as plans crumble,
A, B, C to Z disintegrate.
Chaos, dis-ease, pain, suffering
bring the wheels to a grinding halt.

When our dirt road aspirations
intersect the water of life
may we shun the selfishness of road rage
dare to dive in and swim with abandon;

riding the current of grace,
swimming from stream to merging river,
wider still the water flows,
merging into eternal oneness.

Blip of destination fades from the screen.
Today's swim becomes its own goal,
sojourners form a constantly-morphing map;
we'll recognize home when we get there together.

Luke 9:1-2 Then Jesus called the twelve together and gave them power and authority over all demons and to cure diseases, 2 and he sent them out to proclaim the kingdom of God and to heal.

Graduation

It's a "from" and "to" event;
corner turned on a long journey
neither beginning nor end;
measuring place for future reference.

The "from" is quite obvious to see,
emblazoned in all its academic glory
on framed sheepskin document:
talisman to unlock doors to come.

"To" is equally oblivious, even to you:
plans and dreams laid and envisioned,
timetables and schedules carefully mapped,
future's fluidity refuses to hold any shape
but twists and turns of the river of life itself.

Some fine day when breath-catching

becomes significant enough to warrant practice,
you'll sit and view the map of where
you've been and where you still hope to go.

There on the earlier part of the journey,
map-spot marked by
mortar board, gown, tassel, diploma,
it'll seem so long ago in years and wisdom.

All along the river's journey,
rapids, eddies, gentle currents
buoyed by prayers, grace, hope;
currented by a mix of plans and providence.
"From" always home; "To" forever around the next bend.

Dare to dream your biggest dreams;
give to them the breath of life;
chase them with your heart;
change the world one prayer at a time.

Know you've been sent forth
with all that can be shared,
sewn together with the thread
of God's amazing love and care.

Godspeed!

Genesis 32:30-31 So Jacob called the place Peniel, saying, "For I have seen God face to face, and yet my life is preserved." 31 The sun rose upon him as he passed Penuel, limping because of his hip.

WMDs

Words, the stealth-like weapons
we can unleash with relative ease,
whose half-life far exceeds plutonium,
exacting force for generations to come.

Mass, not just the orthodox celebration
of Eucharist-focused worship,
but also measurable weight and
an overarching sense of totality.

Destruction, the dismantling
of that which has been constructed,
without the least concern for
design, purpose, material, or inhabitants.

We are forever facing two extremes:
"I couldn't help but let that out!" and
"I'll never let you forget you did!"
Both of which enlarge the chasm.

Somewhere in the darkness lie
a tongue well-bitten,
a conversation purposefully forgotten,
hands of grace extended, embraced.

As morning finally arrives,
we will recognize its presence when
forgiveness is as fully self-accepted
as it is freely other-given.

Until that first light shines,
we can only limp away,
Jacob-like from our Peniel,
ever-seeking the face of God.

Ecclesiastes 3:11 He has made everything beautiful in its time. He has also set eternity in the human heart; yet no one can fathom what God has done from beginning to end. (NIV)

Heartbeat

Somewhere, life terminates:
flatline silence, electrical neutrality.
With that ending, family, friends
bid farewell; raw grief protrudes.

How, in this cold, dark pall
can strangers ask for life,
can mourners think, feel beyond self?
Only God can answer.

Years of academic, clinical preparation,
teams of seamless precision
pour out methodical passion,
battling time's incessant beat.

Who's to say what connections weave
when one body merges with another,

one family's loss becomes another's gain?
Time's passing may reveal glimpses.

Have you ever stopped to consider
how this mirrors resurrection;
just might represent the way
God intends the universe to function?

Luke 22:19-20 Then he took a loaf of bread, and when he had given thanks, he broke it and gave it to them, saying, "This is my body, which is given for you. Do this in remembrance of me." 20 And he did the same with the cup after supper, saying, "This cup that is poured out for you is the new covenant in my blood.

Given

Grace is not just
the gift we've been given;
it's also the given
with which we've been gifted;

universal truth delivered

to the whole earth,
wrapped in elemental reality.

It is holy nakedness
allowing us to fully exist
without regard to expectations -
ours or others' – neither needing
to be more or different,
nor shrinking from the sacred whole
that lies within each one;

fully accepting all failed attempts
of self and other to carry
and deliver its precious meal,
yet never settling until Eucharist's
broken, blessed, poured, and shared
promise is finally fulfilled in the flesh.

2 Corinthians 5:7 "For we walk by faith and not by sight."

Faith and Sight

The contrast between
faith and sight takes on
a whole new meaning with
optic malfunction crashing your party.

Yesterday's expectations
threaten to crash and burn;
tomorrow's dreams interrupted by
nightmare of undetermined veracity, duration.

Stepping into, onto darkness,
holding on come hope or high water,
walking toward the dawn.

Jeremiah 29:11's rope swings:

"For I know the plans I have for you,"
declares the Lord, "plans to
prosper you and not to harm you,
plans to give you hope and a future."

Riding shotgun, pirate patched,
praying for courage to let go,
falling into the depths of Grace's river,
floating in your strong, tender palm.

Psalm 124:2-4 if it had not been the Lord who was on our side, when our enemies attacked us, 3 then they would have swallowed us up alive, when their anger was kindled against us; 4 then the flood would have swept us away, the torrent would have gone over us;

Volcanic Grace

Forgiveness flows like molten lava
oozing down the face of life's mountain
melting, shaping, transforming as it goes
consuming lesser gods of pain, anger, vengeance.

From time to time the flow is halted;
coolness by way of distance from Divine,
lesser god rises up to virgin sacrifice,
steeled will releases glacier's ice cap.

Old wounds are lifted high above the flow
preventing their transforming melt;
sufficiently cooled and distanced,
they form a scarring plaque of obstruction.

Beneath the surface, pressure builds,
cooling cap hangs on for hell or high water,

grace's fire may be diverted for a while
but it will not be halted forever.

Through cracks and fissures, steam escapes
hinting at a power that lies beneath;
delayed eruption surprises all in its path
offering hope but not guarantee.

Somewhere along the way
volcano's keeper must decide
to dare lowering long-held pain
into lava's transforming flow.

Telescoped observers on distant peaks
can see so clearly how to proceed,
but only those who've lived the mountain
can feel the heat and take the risk.

Lava's source of unending grace
pleads but will not use force;
surrendered will sets off a chain
of cauterized healing that leads to joy.

1 Kings 17:17-18 After this the son of the woman, the mistress of the house, became ill; his illness was so severe that there was no breath left in him. 18 She then said to Elijah, "What have you against me, O man of God? You have come to me to bring my sin to remembrance, and to cause the death of my son!"

Pediatric Wing

A prayer holds children, high but secure
in hands open and strengthened by practice
up in the sky, above where giraffes forage
to the place where God's vision rests.
The hands are silent, but their voice calls out
"See here! See these children of your own making!
See their parents, siblings, friends, neighbors."

At this altitude, air is thin and breathing measured;
trade-off for the solid security of sea-level;
but there are alternative forms of oxygenation:
rainbow breaths that infuse spirits, fuel imagination;
screens where dreams can replay over and over,
feeding on prayers, promises, power.

The silent voice of uplifted hands demands more than vision;
memory, too, and covenant are part of the plaintive call.
"This is not the 'Do not be afraid.' of your surprise intrusion;
it is the antithesis: the summons for you to boldly arrive into
the midst of the fear, anger, and confusion;
the plea from all who are aware, to sense your presence,
feel your comfort, especially here amidst the chaos."

"Answers seem to be what we want,
but seldom what we receive.
Take what spills from our deep places:
rage, fright, disbelief, despair;
know that we direct it toward you because
you are the one who already knows–
one whose love for us cannot be diminished by it.

Give us what we need: strength for the hour's tasks,
courage not to flinch in anguish's face,
hope that darkness will not– cannot overcome,
light to show at least the next step on the journey,
attentiveness to the joy of each moment,
peace that passes understanding,
new breath to fill us in these thin places."

Psalm 130: 5 I wait for the Lord, my whole being waits, and in his word I put my hope.

Distillery

When fathomless places of another
spill out onto my being,
causing deep to soak to deep,
there comes a time and place
when feelings just won't keep.

Words with their emotions pour
onto napkin, keyboard, page,
leave impressions on my being:
overwhelming joy, grief, outrage.

Word piles into line and verse,
first in droves but then
descending; much more terse.

Until the end is finally found,
and all that's left upon the ground:

a single line of hope, distilled.

John 19:41-42 Now there was a garden in the place where he was crucified, and in the garden there was a new tomb in which no one had ever been laid. 42 And so, because it was the Jewish day of Preparation, and the tomb was nearby, they laid Jesus there.

Garden

Creation began in a garden, O God,
as did Resurrection.
And now we have taken
the blooming flowers of
our own and other gardens
and placed them on a cross
to remind us that we are all your gardeners.

We dig with our hands,
we plant in our hearts,

we water with our tears.
We wait for life to scatter
its pungent fertilizer – its refuse.

We wait for you to send your Son.
And new life is raised up;
raised up in places we had given up for dead;
raised up in places we didn't know existed;
raised up in lives we wouldn't
have given you two cents for.

You've heard us speak the names
and verbalize the circumstances
that frighten us most;
the people and places where
resurrection hope is sorely needed.

Show us this day, and
every day of our lives,
glimpses of your
unimaginable resurrection power,
so we may live as fully Eastered people;
revealing your grace now
and to all generations forevermore.

Luke 4:17-19 and the scroll of the prophet Isaiah was given to him. He unrolled the scroll and found the place where it was written: 18 "The Spirit of the Lord is upon me, because he has anointed me to bring good news to the poor. He has sent me to proclaim release to the captives and recovery of sight to the blind, to let the oppressed go free, 19 to proclaim the year of the Lord's favor."

Freedom

I'm not talking about
romanticized patriotism
that sheds a tear
at Memorial Day parades,
but cannot set aside vested interest
long enough to see
the eye-log terrorism of selfishness.

I'm not talking about
glorified nationalism
that waves a flag
and wins elections,

but has little concern
for the personal lives of ordinary people
who look, speak, or reside in a place
different from us.

I am talking about
deep-to-the-core connectedness
rooted in God-reflection;
single-choice relinquishment
to a plan so large and loving
that new freedoms continually sprout,
surprising us with their tenacity,
gracing us with their joy.

I am talking about
the only freedom
that starts with giving up
perceived freedom of choice and self-will,
and leads to the genuine articles
of sacred breath, holy words,
active participation in the dance
of God's eternal dream.

Job 12: 10 In his hand is the life of every living thing and the breath of every human being.

Everlasting Hope

The breath of life itself is at stake here, O God;
shuttle that transports oxygen to work
and brings carbon dioxide home
after an exhausting "day."

Somewhere in the midst of this bodily function
we try to identify your gift to humanity—
the thing toward which we all aspire;
the gift with which you inspire.

Spirit, breath, wind:
all part of divine inspiration
that claims us as your own, O Lord.

And then the "C" word rears its ugly head,
stepping outside the bounds of cell's cycle,
refusing to yield, hell-bent on growth,
damn the torpedoes-- full speed ahead.

Our plea is for you to intervene,
through medicine or miracle.
Bring your healing touch.
Show us the hem of your garment.
Our arms are outstretched.
Let mercy triumph once more.

As pulse elevates and anxiety rises,
give us pause to notice our own respiration;
give us focus to appreciate both the gift
and the calming effect of its slow and deep practice.

Let us feel, in strong, measured intake,
your comforting promise.
In exhalation, give us release
from all that we cannot control or understand.

Wrap us and those we hold dear
in the swaddling grasp
of your everlasting hope;
through Jesus Christ our Lord.

James 3:17-18 But the wisdom from above is first pure, then peaceable, gentle, willing to yield, full of mercy and good fruits, without a trace of partiality or hypocrisy. 18 And a harvest of righteousness is sown in peace for those who make peace.

Into the Terror

Tiny band of little people,
separated, not as cream from milk,
but night from day;
angry about what is and isn't,
fearful of what's next,
wagering against all hope,
expecting less as victor.

Hatred on a short fuse,
mistrust fully wired,
xenophobia amped to max,
sacrificial lives dehumanized,
calculating rage's dispersion, contagion,
betting on proliferation.

Surprised, overwhelmed, suffocated
by destruction's carnage, intensity;
help arrives from four corners:
order, compassion begin,
Gilead's balm overflows.

Sorting through rubble,
ferreting life's meaning,
forced inventory of value,
prioritizing future's map.

Defining moments like waves,
lap our shores methodically,
tumbling smooth jagged edges.

God only knows who will triumph:
terror's disconnect or holy's hope.

Just in: Love wins?

Psalm 38:6-8 I am bowed down and brought very low; all day long I go about mourning. 7 My back is filled with searing pain; there is no health in my body. 8 I am feeble and utterly crushed; I groan in anguish of heart. (NIV)

Pain

Through the body it runs amuck
dancing its torturous percussion,
laughing in the face of prescriptions,
sneering at all forms of physical therapy.

Left in its wake an exhaustion-numbed mind;
journeys not taken, pleasures forgone,
conversations halted mid-grimace,
person held hostage, life interrupted

Surgery looms ahead in the distance;
another promise piled on the heap.
Dare we let expectation out of the barn
risking another opportunity for deflation?

Welcome sign of Dante's hell
aptly describes daily life.
Hope abandoned, her wares piled high;

shrinking entryway to each succeeding day.

Existential question rears its cumbersome head
posing pain's long-suffering query:
Where and how does God fit into
a life of grief-filled agony?

Isaiah's suffering servant tries to hint
of messianic things to come;
ordinary flesh yields incarnation,
tabernacling Christ has pitched his tent.

What good is that as anesthetic
for folks whose sense of abandonment
is full-grown fanged and neck-chain strong,
daring even the bravest soul to open the gate?

With quivering heart, trembling voice,
past failures openly acknowledged,
words of comfort in short supply,
gate is opened anyway.

Eyes that see and ears that hear,
hands that hold and tears that roll.
Silence open to pain itself,
presence is the initial gift.

We dare to go and place ourselves
at the intersection of pain and life,
hoping to be still and attentive long enough
to experience God's realm close at hand.

Psalm 118:24 This is the day that the Lord has made; let us rejoice and be glad in it.

A Holy Week

As Monday's chaotic start jumps from
underneath the bed like a jack-in-the-box,
may we remember the blessing of
resurrection we are offered each week.

When Tuesday's routine settles in, and
our economic system or our educational process attempt to
convince us of their supremacy, may we
remember the viva la difference of
God's education and economy and be
moved to live toward them.

As Wednesday's hump rolls around, and
our social schedule turns its screws of
angst into our flesh, may we

remember the ultimate freedom and gift of
our membership in the community of the resurrected one.

When Thursday's Doctor appointment
brings us news of dread and fear
may we remember Immanuel, who
tabernacled among us, full of
grace and truth, and was raised
from the dead so that we may experience
resurrection; may we breathe deeply,
inhaling God's hope and promise,
exhaling our own fear and anxiety.

As Friday's pardon sets us free from
the grindstone of worth, may we
find healthful ways to celebrate our
being and not just our doing.

When Saturday's respite brings with it a call to
submit ourselves to an alternative form of
productive worth— be it in the yard, in the house, or elsewhere—
may we remember that we have been
claimed by baptism, nourished for
the weekly journey at the table of grace,
and given the gift of Resurrection so that
we can find our way back to
corporate worship's blessing for another Sunday.

Ruth 1:16 And Ruth said, Intreat me not to leave thee, or to return from following after thee: for whither thou goest, I will go; and where thou lodgest, I will lodge: thy people shall be my people, and thy God my God. (KJV)

Whither Thou Goest

Would that our speech was still
so full of color, but then
we might also be stuck with
such a worldview and
barbaric treatment for
classes and peoples deemed lower.

It is a promise of the highest order,
spoken in the midst of a strange redeeming,
where land and mouths to feed

seem to be of greater import than
emotions and relationships.

Ruth, the outsider of outsiders,
Moabite that she is,
throws ethnicity to the wind
and pledges her troth to a mother-in-law
who is as good as dead.

It's really the pledge of all
who abandon self for the sake of God;
home and kin, vocation and comfort,
all tossed into the whirlwind
of God's tempestuous travel plans.

Who knows how many times
it has been used to caulk wedding vows,
betrothed cleaving themselves one to another?

I do not claim to understand
the mystery of enduring matrimony,
but it does seem to me that when
both partners are willing to live
(not just speak) "Whither thou goest…"
first to God and then to each other,
the grace not only of longevity
but also of joy is within their reach.

Isaiah 7:14 Therefore the Lord himself will give you a sign. Look, the young woman is with child and shall bear a son, and shall name him Immanuel.

Beginning of Advent

'Twas the beginning of Advent and all through the Church
our hope was dying — we'd given up on the search.
It wasn't so much that Christ wasn't invited,
but after 2,000-plus years we were no longer excited.

Oh, we knew what was coming — no doubt about that.
And that was the trouble — it was all "old hat."
November brought the first of an unending series of pains
with carefully orchestrated advertising campaigns.

There were gadgets and dolls and all sorts of toys;
enough to seduce the most devout girls and boys.
Unfortunately, it seemed, no one was completely exempt
from this seasonal virus that did all of us tempt.

The priests and prophets and certainly the kings
were all so consumed with the desire for "things!"
It was rare, if at all, that you'd hear of the reason

for the origin and meaning of this holy-day season.

A baby, it seems, once had been born
in the mid-east somewhere – the first holy-day morn.
But what does that mean for folks like us,
who've lost ourselves in the hoopla and fuss?

Can we re-learn the art of wondering and waiting,
of hoping and praying, and anticipating?
Can we let go of all the things and the stuff?
Can we open our hands and our hearts long enough?

Can we open our eyes and open our ears?
Can we find him again after all of these years?
Will this year be different from all the rest?
Will we be able to offer him all of our best?

So many questions, unanswered thus far,
as wise ones seeking the home of the star.
Where do we begin-- how do we start
to make for the child a place in our heart?

Perhaps we begin by letting go
of our limits on hope, and of the things that we know.
Let go of the shopping, of the chaos and fuss;
let go of the searching, let Christmas find us.

We open our hearts, our hands and our eyes,
to see the king coming in our own neighbors' cries.
We look without seeking what we think we've earned,
but rather we're looking for relationships spurned.

With him he brings wholeness and newness of life
for brother and sister, for husband and wife.
The Christ-child comes not by our skill,
but rather he comes by the Creator's will.

We can't make him come with parties and bright trees,

but only by getting down on our knees.
He'll come if we wait amidst our affliction,
Coming in spite of, and not by our restriction.

His coming will happen-- of this there's no doubt.
The question is whether we'll be in or out.
"Behold, I stand at the door and knock."
Do you have the courage to peer through the lock?

A basket on your porch, a child in your reach.
a baby to love, to feed and to teach.
He'll grow in wisdom as God's only Son.
How far will we follow this radical one?

He'll lead us to challenge the way that things are.
He'll lead us to follow a single bright star.
But that will come later if we're still around.
The question for now: Is the child to be found?

Can we block out commercials, the hype and the malls?
Can we find solitude in our holy halls?
Can we find hope, keep alert, stay awake?
Can we receive the child for ours and God's sake?

From on high with the caroling host as he sees us,
He yearns to read on our lips the prayer: Come Lord Jesus!
As Advent begins, all these questions make plea.
The only true answer: We will see, we will see.

2 Corinthians 5:18-19 All this is from God, who reconciled us to himself through Christ, and has given us the ministry of reconciliation; 19 that is, in Christ God was reconciling the world to himself, not counting their trespasses against them, and entrusting the message of reconciliation to us.

Unreconciled

Time doesn't heal all wounds.
It doesn't even lessen
the grief of some of them.
Mostly, it plods along unceasingly.

Pains have a way of being buried,
when we turn our focus away,
toward something more pleasant,
or at least more pressing.

One day we wake up and find
the opportunity has passed
for healing's words and feelings;
nothing left to do but hurt.

Reconciliation's steady rhythm
will not be drowned out
by distance, time, or death;
the heart of hope forever beats.

We thought it was safely interred,
the "X" spot map long-shredded;
along comes another word or act,
re-opening the dying place within.

Suffering returns with a vengeance,
quickly making up for lost time,
slicing deep into the skin of others,
pulling them into the carnage.

Beyond the sharp vituperation,
beneath the emotional train wreck,
beats a heart with hope forgotten,
longing to trust, to love again.

Spectators to the drama cannot act
to reroute the speeding locomotives,
their only task to mirror the unconditionality
which mercy offers to us all.

Time doesn't heal all wounds,
but it is the place where we survive
while God's reconciling grace
conjures living out of dying.

John 3:34 For the one whom God has sent speaks the words of God, for God gives the Spirit without limit.

Puzzle's Pieces

"God has a plan" we're told
at every twist and turn.
When I stop to look and listen
I sometimes catch a glimpse.

Not enough to figure out
why our lives are full of hurt,
much less the way things
are working together and out.

Seven billion, the last number
I heard used to name the count
of earth's people currently alive,
so maybe we're all part of a puzzle

with that many pieces to fit together.
This doesn't even begin to include
all those who've passed before us:
pieces of the communion of saints.

But since we're being honest here –
which poetry has a way of doing
with few words to hide behind
and truth erupting from its vast blank space –

I must confess that, most of the time,
I find myself imagining a much smaller puzzle,
a 10 or 20 piece version whose box reads,
"Six months to one year."

Is that how long it'll take me to finish,
or how old (mature?) I'm acting,
or the limits of my vision?
Some days it seems like all three.

In this much smaller puzzle, of course,
as intimate and manageable as it is,
I am always the central, most important piece,
in the same way that channelers

always reach back into our past
and find that, once upon a time,
we were, of course, royalty,
and never lower-caste peasants.

But as the universe's true size and age
sink into my dense gray matter,
I sometimes ponder its enormity
that might as well be infinity.

Suppose I am merely—
and I say "merely", because
I'm thinking small and selfishly again—

a tiny piece of gorgeous blue sky

that fits into a few million other blues
to reflect absolute beauty
and not a coveted corner piece
or the iris of a gorgeous eye?

How many times do you think
that eyes roll and sighs flow from God,
exasperated that I'm looking to become
anything and everything except

the very thing for which I was created?
Not that my piece of the puzzle
is not placed in a single right location—
the only spot that it correctly fits—

but that I refuse altogether
to let it fit in any of the many places
it might have twisted and clicked
to fill a hole in the universe's scheme

which my absence makes so obvious.
On my computer the other day
I saw a large image that, from far away,
looked like nothing more

than a single, familiar celebrity's face.
But when I clicked on any given spot
it zoomed to reveal each pixel patch
composed of many other faces.

Funny how easily we can be convinced
by fear, anxiety, envy and control,
that our own comfortable little perspective
must be THE true universal reality.

Matthew 2:11 On entering the house, they saw the child with Mary his mother; and they knelt down and paid him homage. Then, opening their treasure chests, they offered him gifts of gold, frankincense, and myrrh.

Remind Us

Remind us, O God,
that the real question is not,
"Where were you when
the world stopped turning
that September day?"
but "Where have you been
since then, and who are you now?"

Remind us that the quickest way
for terror to win is for hatred,
fear, anxiety, and xenophobia to flourish.

Remind us that terror will be defeated
when understanding, hope, education,
peace, and love triumph.

Remind us that grace is the gift
we have been given
to bring to the struggle.

Genesis 34:5 Now Jacob heard that Shechem had defiled his daughter Dinah; but his sons were with his cattle in the field, so Jacob held his peace until they came.

Shattered

Violation shatters all pretense
of order and ordinary, shocking us
into anger that boils the heart;
an abomination beyond boiling
a kid in its mother's milk (EX 23:19).

Let our rage burn not just your ears,
O God, but also your sense of justice!
Vengeance, the only item on our menu;
hatred, the weed overwhelming our garden.

Give us courage to trust your providence,
tenderness to recognize your presence in the dark,
wisdom to acquiesce to your retribution.

Grant us the redemption of your healing,
the hope of your promised restoration,

the grace of our own resurrection now!

Mark 5:41 He took her by the hand and said to her, "Talitha cum," which means, "Little girl, get up!"

Miracles

Miracles seem to happen
amidst anxious pleas from those
who, by love, are overwhelmed
to the point of desperation.

Who's to say how, why, when
the power of love will easter-up
in places we never could have dreamed,
yet to whose possibility we cling
as castaways to a lone sliver of flotsam?

Who's to know how long before,
or if, major chunks and parts
of who we are, once lost,
can now be found?

We are left with what we see,
praising God that in our midst
new life has been counted.

Let us dare not deceive ourselves;
miracles are not for our sakes alone,

but that grace forever flow, everywhere!

Psalm 139: 13-15 For it was you who formed my inward parts; you knit me together in my mother's womb. 14 I praise you, for I am fearfully and wonderfully made. Wonderful are your works; that I know very well. 15 My frame was not hidden from you, when I was being made in secret, intricately woven in the depths of the earth.

Eviction Notice

O Lord, you know the human body better
than anyone or anything, because
'twas you that knit us together when
we, ourselves, came into this world.

The nature of life and of birth is
set within our genetic matter and
connects us back to that first pool that
bubbled onto this third rock's surface.

Gestation has its course and mostly runs it,
except for those times when something
goes wrong – we know not what – and
upsets the very yin and yang of existence.

But you gave us more than hormones and

animal instincts to work with;
you gave us intangibles of faith, hope, trust,
and even that great mystery we tame with "love."

Our faith won't let us sit still;
our hope won't allow us to let go;
our trust won't relinquish creation's dust to dust;
we must beseech you – call to you.

Give this child a fighting chance;
grant her a stay of gestational eviction
so that her lungs might better prepare to give and
take the very breath of life from your spirit.

Grant her mother your peace that
passes understanding so that
rest may come, and the whir and beep of machines—
the flashing of lights may signal
a cease fire in the battle of labor.

We, who wait and pray with all the fervor
we can muster, ask you to remember
your rainbow promise and take away
this flood of terror that threatens us.

John 20:19 When it was evening on that day, the first day of the week, and the doors of the house where the disciples had met were locked for fear of the Jews, Jesus came and stood among them and said, "Peace be with you."

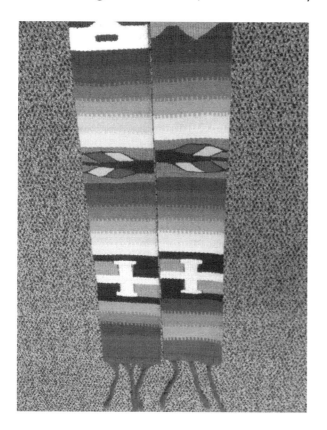

Resurrection

Nearly all the disciples gave up
within three days of the terror;
fishermen back to their boats,
Cleopas and another to Emmaus.

"We had hoped…" they said,
perhaps unaware of the deflating protrusion
of the past-tense helping verb "had"
and the way their yearning for "normal"

even though normal could never be the same,
seemed to close the door on possibility.
But hope, and certainly God,
never had much need for doors,

or windows either, for that matter.
Because even when the doors are locked
for fear—no matter what fear—
resurrection has a way of slipping in anyway.

It doesn't come because we demand it,
won't arrive because we deserve it,
refuses to yield to the "earners".
It just decides to blow in like the wind.

Seldom in a hurry or on our schedule,
often in nearly invisible increments,
physical at times, but always apt
to be emotional, relational, too,

because it is in our connections—
our common human stories—
that we so desperately need to find
the healing power of grace:

forgiveness for imperfections and pain caused;
mercy for frequent self-absorption;
understanding for fear and hiding;
love that binds everything together.

Genesis 3:19 By the sweat of your face you shall eat bread until you return to the ground, for out of it you were taken; you are dust, and to dust you shall return."

Scattering

Ashes to ashes, dust to dust;
our beginning and our end
are one and the same.

From the earth's clay, God formed us
on the universe's pottery wheel;
and when our shape and form were pleasing,
into us God breathed wind and Spirit.

Her living was like ours:
a beginning in which we play no part;
an expanse in the middle filled with
expectations, hopes, dreams,
work, play, suffering, joy;
an end that catches us all by surprise.

As we scatter these ashes into the wind,
may they blow to the four corners of the universe

offering us guidance through
our own wilderness and chaos.

As ashes sink into the moving river,
flowing toward the ever-expansive gulf
that empties into the great sea of oneness,
may we follow their path with our living,
one day claiming our connection with all of creation.

Grant, O God, that we may
forever carry with us from this place
the love and care we saw and felt in our loved one,
and your peace that passes understanding.

1 Samuel 13:6-7 When the Israelites saw that they were in distress (for the troops were hard pressed), the people hid themselves in caves and in holes and in rocks and in tombs and in cisterns. 7 Some Hebrews crossed the Jordan to the land of Gad and Gilead. Saul was still at Gilgal, and all the people followed him trembling.

Fearing

Control's illusion exposed by flashbulb of reality;
chaos unpacks for indeterminate stay;
pain, suffering, grief yo-yo clock's face;
indigestion settles into body, mind, spirit.

Trust is recliner first rendered unsittable;
peace, the rug rolled up, discarded;
accessories of joy, contentment junked;
hope as decorating scheme, scratched.

Soon, house of grace is unfit dwelling;
security's need overpowers faith's open windows;
living warmth of wood replaced
by immovable, icy tower of steel.

Self's betrayal disperses in all directions,
absorbing, rather than giving off light;

darkness spirals ever-inward;
immobility preferred over toe-stumping, stumbling.

Into this night, peacock cries,
eerie facsimile of innocent child,
restlessly scratching on the roof,
dying, yet living to come in.

Forgiveness approaches as entrepreneur,
refusing to pick lock,
knocking with morning's first rays,
holding tiny sample of unconditional love.

Mercy begins with turned doorknob;
one wall, one piece at a time,
restoration is mysterious reversal toward grace;
fear, the stubborn, final exorcism.

2 Thessalonians 2:15-17 So then, brothers and sisters, stand firm and hold fast to the traditions that you were taught by us, either by word of mouth or by our letter. 16 Now may our Lord Jesus Christ himself and God our Father, who loved us and through grace gave us eternal comfort and good hope, 17comfort your hearts and strengthen them in every good work and word.

Beating Heart

We often forget our own,
pounding away in anonymity;
pumping life throughout
body we push to the limit.

Certain circumstances provoke
pronounced pulsation,
essential tachycardia:
anger, fear, passion.

Other events swing pendulum
180 degrees, slow-motion beat
cold molasses flows faster:
peace, contentment, trust.

What about corporate body,
very flesh of the Christ,
chasing resurrection dreams,
living gospel's challenge?

Where lies church arteriosclerosis,
hardened pathways preventing
life-flow to conversations,
inspiration to visions?

Let us stent congregational arteries:
scripture, prayer, conversation;
vasodilatiors beckoning
toward the path of faith.

Mark 10:15-16 Truly I tell you, whoever does not receive the kingdom of God as a little child will never enter it." 16 And he took them up in his arms, laid his hands on them, and blessed them.

Simple Faith

Childlike faith is what
the recipe calls for;
it might as well be eye of newt or
some other such exotic ingredient.

Who can measure or identify
the hope of juvenile purity?
Who could ever hope to
replicate such a ghost
long after innocence becomes
a casualty of time and experience?

In the face of youth we see only
inexperience, naiveté, even foolishness;
vulnerability, risk, trust go
unnoticed, unappreciated, unheralded.

Ingredientless, clueless, desperate,
we press on, substituting at will,
frantically mixing, stirring,
wishing for a miracle.

Childlike's depth bows to
simplicity's breadth;
trust's patience gives way to
fear's pounding chorus;
possibility succumbs to ought.

Unexamined piety's anger
chills the soul;
crusts another layer
of resentment between
one heart and another.

Where, O Lord, are the children?
Why can't we make our way
back to their innocent treasure,
to their vulnerable leap?

John 1:38-39a When Jesus turned and saw them following, he said to them, "What are you looking for?" They said to him, "Rabbi" (which translated means Teacher), "where are you staying?" 39a He said to them, "Come and see."

Come and See

"Come and see."
says the spider to the fly.
"Reach out and touch my web,
and you will surely die."

"Come and see."
says the serpent to Ms. Eve.
"The fruit that makes you God,
will also make you leave."

"Come and see."
says El to Abram's clan.
"I don't even have a map,
just a daily travel plan."

"Come and see."
says I-AM to shepherd Mose.

"My fire has made the dirt
sacred to your very toes."

"Come and see."
says Yahweh to Pharaoh.
"The sea will wash away
remnants of your ego."

"Come and see."
says Dave to Philistia's giant.
"I'll rock your soul to sleep
and make your troops compliant."

"Come and see."
says Jesus to John's guys.
"The kingdom has arrived.
See with your own eyes."

"Come and see."
says the woman at the well.
"The source of Living Water
did my life's story tell."

"Come and see."
the gospel calls us now.
"Dare to let completely go.
Story shows you how."

"Come and see."
the Spirit whispers low.
"I'll set your soul on fire,
and then God's wind will blow."

"Come and see."
is all we have to say;
a three word invitation
to show others the way.

"Come and see
the way our lives have changed.
Our plans and expectations
are by God now rearranged."

"Come and see.
It's the only way to grow
into the very beings
who're both known by God and know."

Psalm 42:3 My tears have been my food day and night, while people say to me continually, "Where is your God?"

Silence

Death has its own way
of affecting vocal chords,
not only in those it takes
but in the rest of us, too.

No matter how often we taste
its bitter-herbed fare
the swallowing is still hard
and sorely shocks our palate.

Pleased that its arrival
has rocked our world again,
Death sets out to score
a permanent victory.

Knowing that the voices
are how we measure life,
it plays upon our fears
of grave's silent echo.

It hopes we'll quickly scramble,
filling the auditory void
with whatever ramblings
our random files submit.

But when the platitudes have faded
and left us empty caloried,
silence comes out of hiding
and pleads for our presence.

Sit and be with me for a while
as our ears seek respite so that
our hearts can taste the whisper
of sorrow's bittersweet sustenance.

Luke 2: 50-51 But they did not understand what he said to them. 51 Then he went down with them and came to Nazareth, and was obedient to them. His mother treasured all these things in her heart.

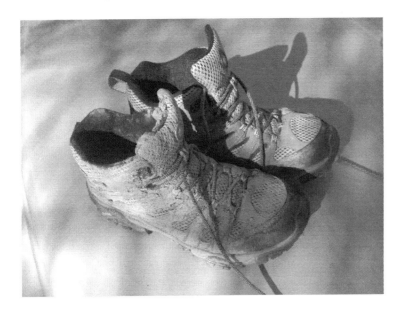

All Who Wonder

All who wonder are not lost
unless you count being found by God
as the total loss of control it truly is.

When fear gives way to curiosity,
all hope for individuation flies
the way of first naiveté.

But oh, the joy of life unleashed
when, held in God's mysterious palm,
we uncork life's champagne questions!

The who and how of our connection
weaves intergenerational tapestry
as universal quilt of hope.

Me and thee, I and thou
become the "us" of universe;
things used, people loved.

Grain, grape, water morph
from ordinary, daily sustenance
to sacramental grace.

World shrinks without claustrophobia,
stories blend without consuming,
love wins without suffocating.

Job 2:12-13 When they saw him from a distance, they did not recognize him, and they raised their voices and wept aloud; they tore their robes and threw dust in the air upon their heads. 13 They sat with him on the ground seven days and seven nights, and no one spoke a word to him, for they saw that his suffering was very great.

How Much?

Not just, "How long"? but
"How much can one family take?"
When the "C" Reaper circles
the block, over and over,
faith is hard pressed to
maintain its full-bodied flavor.

We cry in the closet sometimes,
trying to be strong for others,
because that's what we think
we're supposed to do.

But you, O Lord, have created us
for community, for each other,
and if there's any time we need
each other more than ever,

surely it is now!

Surround us with the love
of those who can and will
sing the songs of faith for us,
recite the creeds on our behalf,
believing for us, for a while,
until we can breathe again.

As much as we think we want to
see and understand the big picture,
what we'd really like right now
is to change the smaller picture,
re-pixeling the molecular details
of our very beings until
normal returns from its exile.

Into your hands, O God,
we commend our lives,
our love, our souls.
Hear our cries and answer us.
Hold us with the fierce but tender care
of a mother's and father's love;
breathe into us your life that is sustained
now and forevermore.

Matthew 28:18-20 And Jesus came and said to them, "All authority in heaven and on earth has been given to me. 19 Go therefore and make disciples of all nations, baptizing them in the name of the Father and of the Son and of the Holy Spirit, 20 and teaching them to obey everything that I have commanded you. And remember, I am with you always, to the end of the age."

Go and Serve

"Go and serve" said El to Abraham.
"Follow my lead and I will
make your descendants exceed
the number of the stars."

Abraham used all his wit and guile
to help God's promise come true,
but finally had to sit back and laugh
as God made the impossible possible.

"Go and serve" said God
to Jacob's eleventh son.

"Your dreams will take you to the very place
where you can serve me best."

From the pit, to Potiphar's, to prison,
Joseph dreamed his way
into Pharaoh's court.

"Go and serve" said I-AM
to Moses at the burning bush.
"I'll take your halting voice and
your flaring temper, and use them
to stage an unparalleled deliverance."

Forty years later, Moses handed
Joshua the water-parting reins
of a newly formed nation at Jericho.

"Go and serve" said Jesus to the crowds.
"Take the hunger-abating, thirst-quenching,
disease-healing, disability-destroying
power that you have seen, experienced, and received;
turn it loose in the places where
you work, play, live, and breathe.

And here we still gather, again and again,
to praise and worship the God
who bids us to "Go and serve."

Romans 8: 14-16 For all who are led by the Spirit of God are children of God. 15 For you did not receive a spirit of slavery to fall back into fear, but you have received a spirit of adoption. When we cry, "Abba! Father!" 16 it is that very Spirit bearing witness with our spirit that we are children of God...

Go Gently

Much of culture demands we fight,
tooth and nail against going,
denying that we're even moving in that direction,
color for the fading hair,
tucks and injections for the sags and wrinkles.

Fight whatever comes our way
with whatever we can arm ourselves:
radical surgery, medicine, harsh treatment, equipment;
all ways to deny journey's inevitability,
pretending we can park indefinitely.

There is another way to travel,
not so much upstream always,
not eternally against traffic's flow,
but putting up our sail and
letting breath blow us where it will.

A toast to all who find the grace
to tread gingerly upon the earth,
softly upon other lives so that
breathing comes as if from Spirit,
flowers bloom at every turn:

May you go gently toward the place
where earth gives way to garden,
where hope is planted, not buried,
where time stretches into infinity,
and living yields willingly to eternity.

Genesis 25:8 Abraham breathed his last and died in a good old age, an old man and full of years, and was gathered to his people.

Fading Light

Creator of the universe's height, depth, breadth;
awe in the presence of your glory; amazement
in the face of your immense creation;
knee-struck our repose, silence our response.

But you are more than distant power,
closer than spangled heavens, more intimate
than unmoved mover; you are Incarnation,
breath of life itself; you are here and now.

Of all we gather from our storied past –
all we can retell of history and hope –
suffering does not bring your retreat;
death's knell fails to send you scurrying for cover.

Would that we could understand
the how and why of it all;
wisdom as deliverance from self-absorption is

hard to squeeze from grief's breathlessness.

Grant us relief from pain's intensity, peace that
passes understanding, courage to face the edge
of earth and sky as those whose faith mortars
the vast expanse between tiny bricks of understanding.

Show us your presence in the tightly drawn
face of pain; reflect your shalom in
the pool of compassion; let us feel your touch
in hands whose healing is release.

Matthew 6:22 Your eyes are windows into your body. If you open your eyes wide in wonder and belief, your body fills up with light. (The Message)

The Eyes Have It

Dare we look into each other's eyes?
Perhaps for a brief moment only;
long enough to convey sincerity,
dispelling any notion of deceit.

For if the ancients are correct,
iris reflecting iris just might reveal
more about me than I want you to know,
more about you than I am ready to receive.

Pain I see looking back at me
begs a pause for deep reflection;
emotional and mental mirroring
daring me to wonder, if only silently

whether the suffering before me
is wholly other, beyond my experience,
or some universal connection,

itself a piece of the holy puzzle.

I am afraid to know and ask,
yet so desperately need to,
because it is not just about
finding out who you are,

but also about me finding out
who I am, and even more,
about me risking my very soul
in letting you in on that reflection.

So when you contemplate locking eyes,
if only at a distance for a moment,
consider what we were before
and whom our eyes may cause us to become.

Exodus 32:12 Why should the Egyptians say, 'It was with evil intent that he brought them out to kill them in the mountains, and to consume them from the face of the earth'? Turn from your fierce wrath; change your mind and do not bring disaster on your people.

Taken

Whenever something precious is taken,
but especially life itself,
we find ourselves inhaling sharply,
yet all the breath in the world
is not able to inflate our spirits
against this violation of theft.

God, the only one
to and against whom
charges can be filed.
Flying in the face of polite society,
file we must.

"Here we are, your children,
at your mercy for even daily bread!
How is it then, that we
are supposed to survive this loss?

Take this our impassioned ire,
drive it into your holy heart,
let its fireworks there erupt.

We can do nothing less
and nothing more ourselves,

until you hope us once again!"

Luke 15:20 So he got up and went to his father. "But while he was still a long way off, his father saw him and was filled with compassion for him; he ran to his son, threw his arms around him and kissed him.

Crossing

Courage for crossing comes
not in bravado's leap toward the abyss
or titanium-willed single-mindedness
or inflated words of assurance or denial.

Courage for crossing comes
not in pain denied, endured, or masked
or physical weakness' regret
or obsessive orderly preparation.

Courage for crossing comes
in turning loose of titles and accomplishments
in joyously answering roll call:
"Welcome home, my precious child."

In memory of L. L. "Bud" Jenkins

Galatians 4:4-5 But when the fullness of time had come, God sent his Son, born of a woman, born under the law, 5 in order to redeem those who were under the law, so that we might receive adoption as children.

Old Flame

In the chronological scheme of things
there is no old flame like the Old Flame;
no one who knows or has been known
longer than the One whose passion

sparked the universe's first fireworks,
sizzling primordial ooze into the ordered
complex universe of double-hydrogenated
oxygen and carbon-based life

that we so conveniently believe to be
our own inalienable right to existence
as if we ourselves had access to
the codes and keys of creation.

In the kairological scheme of things
there is no old flame like the Old Flame;

One who blended body, mind, spirit;
threw in the inexplicability of soul

to plant a seed of mystery at the core
of our very connectedness so that
we would spend our lives sprouting
toward but never fully realizing

unified completeness and being;
bound by ever-ticking chronos
yet forever linked to and drawn toward
the boundless infinity of kairos.

Genesis 23:2 And Sarah died at Kiriath-arba (that is, Hebron) in the land of Canaan; and Abraham went in to mourn for Sarah and to weep for her.

Gray Season

When leaves blowing off of trees
remind us of wheels coming off our lives;
thickening gray of winter presses down
like a too-heavy woolen blanket,

smothering desire to live;
making breath itself a luxury
for which we cannot afford to splurge.
Shortening days and lessened sun's angle

heap cold, saturating fog,
pressing down anything but good measure.
Bone weary, brain worn,
rope grows shorter by the hour.

What were things that gave
meaning to existence?
Where are lights that brought
load-lifting relief?

Hope, misplaced so easily, vanishes
like love letters slipping behind the dresser,
wedged between floor and wall;
their tender intimacies stone-cold mute.

Love securely tethered to one who's gone
has lost its will to soar above
cold molasses drear
of this hell-compressed atmosphere.

Faith that's forced to settle for little more
than knowledge times belief
scarcely pulses enough blood
to raise the wrist's flesh.

Dare we let this hypothermia
reorient our very souls?
Can we run the risk
of starting over—starting grander?

Not a cool disdainful break
from who we are, have become,
refusing to integrate eclectic mess
of all our storied, mismatch baggage;

but rather in a way that gently
gathers all the broken pieces,
integrating them with other
bits of whom we're meant to be

so that hope's parachute opens fully,
faith's yeast rises to a fragrant loaf,
love blossoms strong but tender,
and this gray season is put to rest.

Luke 3:21-22 Now when all the people were baptized, and when Jesus also had been baptized and was praying, the heaven was opened, 22 and the Holy Spirit descended upon him in bodily form like a dove. And a voice came from heaven, "You are my Son, the Beloved; with you I am well pleased."

Core Identity

We live, O God, in this conflicted world;
conflicted with its messages about who we are:
consumer... conqueror... titled... entitled... controller.

We try so hard to operate out of these messages:
consuming... conquering... titling... entitling... controlling.

And yet a voice whispers in the darkness;
whispers of another identity:
forgiven... freed... covenanted....
child of the God who is Father, Son, and Holy Spirit.

And we are reminded of the gift of living this identity:
forgiving... freeing... covenanting... blessing.

It isn't so hard to live this core identity –
this baptismal identity –
while we are gathered in community;
at least as long as we don't
look too closely down our noses
at our baptized brothers and sisters;
and as long as we don't talk or think
about the rest of our lives.

But, oh, Lord, when Monday rolls around
and the rest of the week hammers away,
this gift whispers in public,
on the job... at work... at home;
then we've got trouble
right here in Jordan River City.

The gift has the audacity to claim
that it has something important to say
about our work... our investments...
our unflinching support
of brutality and coercion in all their nasty disguises:
in the military and in the marketplace,
in the boardroom and in the bedroom.

Our baptismal identity dares to raise the specter
of our own support of injustice,
either by our active participation or our passive silence;
and we turn up the volume of the lesser voices;
hoping they will drown out the whisper.

But the whisper will not go away;
its steady cadence like a drum,
resonating deep within;
under... around... and through all others.

O God of baptismal whisper,
shore up our courage as only you can do,
pry open our hearts and ears in your holy power,

strengthen your will in us through your gift of grace,
that we might truly live in the joy
of the core identity claimed for us at baptism;
through Jesus the baptized one.

Psalm 24:1-2 The earth is the Lord's and all that is in it, the world, and those who live in it; 2 for he has founded it on the seas, and established it on the rivers.

Redistribution

Every generation grasps its wealth,
convinced that what's possessed
not only has been obtained by fair means
but done according to divine desire.

Original distribution, then,
took place between the tree of life
and the tree of the knowledge
of good and evil – Eden was its name.

Ever since Cain's possessiveness emerged,
we've redistributed what belongs to God,
as if it were ours alone to keep or give,
warring madness the ultimate distribution struggle.

How long, O Lord, before
we realize again for the first time
that the measure of our success
is not what's won, lost, amassed,

but how we hold onto one another
with strong, tender, open hands;
how we feed our neighbors by
the long-handled spoon of grace?

Matthew 18: 10 "Take care that you do not despise one of these little ones; for, I tell you, in heaven their angels continually see the face of my Father in heaven.

Alternatives

We, as a human race, O God,
are slow to learn that death may not be
the most effective response to hatred,
dehumanization not the most healthy means
of international relations,
and preemption leaves a bit to be desired
as a reaction to terrorism.

When we fail to see the direct correlation
of escalation, somehow blinded by moral superiority,
are we also blind to transforming alternatives?

Help us, O Lord, to seek paths toward peace
that have not been irreparably rutted
by the supply train of war's weaponry.

Help nations to find workable ways
to weave justice together with mercy,

so that innocent life does not become
the debris of international confrontation.

We remember not only the potential casualties
in the civilian population, but also
the thousands of men and women
who have accepted the calling of soldierhood—
those who daily face the front line,
squeezing precious tube of courage,
risking life and limb.

If ever there was a need for guardian angels,
it is on the streets-turned battlefield,
and on the ships, planes, assault vehicles,
tanks, choppers, and in the bunkers......
Send your angels to do your watching,
O God..... send your angels!

Isaiah 55: 8-9 For my thoughts are not your thoughts, nor are your ways my ways, says the Lord. 9 For as the heavens are higher than the earth, so are my ways higher than your ways and my thoughts than your thoughts.

Rekindled

How sad and yet how refreshingly relieving
it will be to discover,
at the edge and earth and sky,
that God has little concern for
the dramas around which
we have not only built our lives,
but also the church.

Imagine dollar bills becoming Kleenex,
real estate converted to Universal Parks,
locks, doors, fences dispensed with altogether.
Worship's jukebox consisting of much more
than the only genre sacred to
our own generation and culture.

Into what will we pour our passion,
when angst over gender-commitments
is exposed for the Middle Garden Fruit that it is,
when our asthmatic understanding of love
is seen in the robust light of day?

To revel in something iota-less,
to stoke the fires of heart and life
with all our deepest inner kindling,
to pray and sing with reckless abandon!

To serve, not for salvation, profit, or praise;
but because it is not within us
to do anything less!

How long, O Lord, will it take
for us to reach the pearly gates?

Why not begin this paradise today?

Matthew 2:1-2 In the time of King Herod, after Jesus was born in Bethlehem of Judea, wise men from the East came to Jerusalem, 2 asking, "Where is the child who has been born king of the Jews? For we observed his star at its rising, and have come to pay him homage."

Dangerous Epiphany

'Twas the day of Epiphany and throughout the kirk
deacons, elders, even pastors were all hard at work.
Birthed in ad nauseam meetings of committees:
a welcome for savior with multiple strategies.

Isaiah and Micah were thoroughly consulted
protocol followed so messiah not insulted.
If truth were told, devoid of fears,
strategy unchanged for thousands of years.

But that didn't matter to movers and shakers
who had long-acquiesced to the few belly-achers.
The church was now running like a well-oiled machine,
even though it no longer remembered the dream.

Just how it happened we can't quite remember,
the only detail: six days past December.
The intercom buzzed: visitors of good cheer;
their accents revealed they were not from around here.

Against better judgment they were ushered inside,
their odor, their aura could not be denied.
Juan Carlos the name of one who sojourned,
then Achmed and Mico. Is your stomach churned?

The more it unfolded the crazier it was,
their story of following a star here because
a promise just born. They knew it was wild,
seeking our guidance to locate this child.

Notify the committee, for a rapid convening;
two items of agenda to discover the meaning
of these moon willow sultans and their way-bizarre tale.
Should we signal panic? Should the alarm siren wail?

Is it immigrant issues or a terrorists plot
that begs us to terminate this plan on the spot?
Cool heads prevail; a subversion is planned
to protect our dear children and our sacred land.

We'll play right along with this ludicrous search
keeping all under wraps to protect state and church.
If indeed they discover this child in our midst,
the S.W.A.T. team will swoop in a lead-blanket blitz.

We'll make the world safe. We'll wipe out the danger,
returning to life minus the stranger;
giving-in to our angst, feeding our fears,
ignoring the Christ whose eyes fill with tears.

Mark 16: 8 So they went out and fled from the tomb, for terror and amazement had seized them; and they said nothing to anyone, for they were afraid.

Breathe Resurrection

We, with Mark's gospel disciples,
seized by terror and amazement;
epic battle between life and death
always leaves us gasping, gaping.

Terror's pulsing hand wraps
around one side of our neck;
other side equally squeezed
by amazement's trembling digits.

Into this place, time, circumstance
resurrection seems only a myth;
comic-book tale filled with
absurdity of rabbits hiding eggs.

With Luke's Emmaus road travelers
"We had hoped..." so many things.
Now it seems we are at the end;
no tools or tricks left up our sleeve.

We, with the 139th psalmist

have been hidden by darkness
for so long we're not sure what
we'll find when "We come to the end…"

You chose sweating flesh, pulsing blood
in which to pitch your tent among us;
our absorption of your grace and truth
inhibited by our angst, outrage.

We, with all the psalmists, story's characters
dare to let the volcano of our pain erupt,
laying blame before you with the courage,
desperation of ammas, abbas preceding.

Enfold us in your tender arms of mercy;
whisper grace's oil into our tear-rusted ears;
show us daybreak flashes of empty tomb;
lead us to the feast of your daily manna.

Author of all our collective narratives,
give us courage to turn unwritten pages,
strength to live into unknown conclusion,
hope to breathe gift of resurrection.

Let us be counted among those
disregarding dignity, breaking into
all-out sprint from the cemetery
to proclaim the Easter promise,
"He is risen! Christ is risen indeed!"

2 Corinthians 9:5 So I thought it necessary to urge the brothers to go on ahead to you, and arrange in advance for this bountiful gift that you have promised, so that it may be ready as a voluntary gift and not as an extortion.

Holy Purpose

As long as our culture
operates by the economy of scarcity
and self-definition via competition,

we will always create an imaginary line
in the measure of productivity
beyond which many people will decide

they are entitled to hoard and hide,
without recognizing the way
this gating defies our holy purpose.

No longer do we have
the understanding that ability
is a gift to be purposed for creation;

instead we find ourselves
privatizing the math of creativity
with no possible factor beyond

the lonely little X of self.
Surrounded by our stuff,
 we devolve into endless appetites.

Lord, help us find our way
back to the table of community
and abundance where none are uninvited!

Romans 12: 11-12 Do not lag in zeal, be ardent in spirit, serve the Lord. 12 Rejoice in hope, be patient in suffering, persevere in prayer.

Bolder Dash

Fear assaults halls of prayer,
intimidates with balderdash,
"What good is petition
if it doesn't come true?"

Reason peeks from behind Anxiety,
calculates known sequencing,
concurs with Fear's assessment,
"Not very likely to happen."

Faith blows in from four corners,
laughs at the absurdity,
"Prayer isn't an exercise in probability;
but rather one of possibility."

Hope musters up from the deeps,
rolls away the stone of doubt,
"It's not really prayer until

it approaches the preposterous!"

Courage starches the sails,
squeezes adrenal glands,
"Now is not the time for timidity;
it's time to make a bolder dash."

Dove descends in fire and cloud,
voice of gentle thunder,
"Unleash your wildest prayers of healing
for those whose faith and hope are fading!"

Ours is not the task
to determine what will or won't,
but to fiercely ask for what we need
and wholly trust the holy Giver.

Scripture Index

Unless otherwise indicated, all Scripture quotations are from the NRSV.

Made in the USA
Charleston, SC
05 June 2014